To all those who have wounded or been wounded in the name of Christ. May you find great freedom and joy in rediscovering church as healthy heart-to-heart connection.

Relational Revolution

5 Shifts for ReDiscovering Church As Heart-to-Heart Connection

John C. White
Toni M. Daniels
Dr. Kent Smith

Relational Revolution

For more information, email community@lk10.com.
ISBN: 978-1-7346840-5-6 (hardback)
ISBN: 978-1-7346840-4-9 (paperback)
Editing by Jim Bryson (JamesLBryson@gmail.com)

Get Your Free Bonuses!

As you read this book we have some bonus resources to help you implement a relational revolution in your network of family and friends—thank you for reading *Relational Revolution.*

Visit LK10.com/bookbonus (or scan the QR code) to access:

A practical video series sharing how leaders like you are living out these 5 shifts in a wide range of church, family and movement contexts.

Our high-impact "Heavy Emotions" tool used daily by facilitators of this revolution. This is a simple PDF that equips you in a Jesus-led, Joy-fueled process for handling heavy emotions as a safe and transformational community.

Scan the QR code, or visit us at:

www.lk10.com/bookbonus

Table of Contents

How This Book Happened 1

Dear Reader, ... 5

What Is God Doing? 7

1. The "Dones" 19

2. Joy Fueled 27

3 .Jesus Led 35

4. Communities of Practice 43

5. Maturing Spiritual Parents 53

6. Nurturing Ecosystems of Grace 65

7. Creating New Culture 75

8. The Invitation From Here… 83

Books Are Okay… 87

Resources and Unique Contributions 89

Acknowledgements 103

Read More 107

Author Bios 109

Would You Review? 115

How This Book Happened

This book is the product of a change in plans. John White and Kent Smith met in 2003. Both men at the time had decades of experience planting and leading churches and training next-generation church leaders. It was clear to them by then that revolutionary change was needed—and coming—in Western church culture.

After collaborating for five years exploring what that kind of culture change could mean, in 2008 they founded LK10. Their purpose was to equip and connect leaders of the coming revolution with the vision of "seeing a vibrant family of Jesus in close reach of everyone, worldwide."

Toni Daniels joined the LK10 leadership in 2015, taking a key role in raising LK10's equipping to new levels of effectiveness in what was by then a growing, worldwide movement. Ten years into LK10's work, these three leaders gathered in Nashville, Tennessee to reflect on the lessons learned and discern the core values that seemed foundational to the impact LK10 was seeing across cultures in dozens of nations.

From that time of reflection together with the Lord, these five core values emerged:

LK10 is a network of:

Joy-fueled
Jesus-Led
Communities of Practice that are equipping
Spiritual Parents to nurture
Ecosystems of Grace.

That is quite a mouthful of unusual values! But, isn't this just what we would expect if, in fact, the realities LK10 was observing were truly revolutionary? Equally clear, though, was that these values would need to be unpacked in plain language for those joining the revolution to make sense of them.

So, the team decided to write five books, one for each of the values. The first of these, *Joy Fueled,* was published in 2020 to wide acclaim and became a best-seller. The next book, *Jesus Led,* was well underway when the team met in person to finish it in 2022. That's when the plans changed.

The team realized that at the current rate, it would be years before all five books could be published. Meanwhile, the positive impacts of LK10's training in many places, across many cultures, were becoming undeniably clear.

Sometimes in the medical world, clinical trials of a new treatment are stopped early, because it becomes so apparent that the treatment is working. When this happens, researchers want the people who are not receiving the treatment to receive it as soon as possible and stop the trial.

On the writing retreat, this was the team's sense—in light of the amazing results LK10 was seeing, now was the time to get the word out as widely as possible about the relational revolution underway in Christian culture. To do this, a short, simple overview of all five core values was the need of the hour.

As John White said, "While we were writing *Jesus Led*, Jesus led us to write another book!"

This book is the product of that guidance. With this background in mind, it is important to say upfront what this book is and what it is not. It is an attempt to state clearly five core values that, in combination, describe a revolution in Christian culture that LK10 is observing as an active participant. *Relational Revolution* offers an overview of this new/old culture and how it contrasts with much that is standard practice in current Christian culture.

What this book is *not* is a comprehensive treatment of the five values and the cultural shifts they represent. It is meant to be more of a declaration than a thorough explanation. For that level of understanding, we have a few recommendations:

Get to know us at LK10.com, where you can sign up for an Introductory Call.

Listen to "Stories from the Revolution" podcast.

Read our books that will explore each core value in detail. *Joy Fueled: Catalyzing a Revolution of Joyful Communities,* the first of these is currently available. To receive notification of upcoming books, contact us at LK10.com/bookupdate.

Meanwhile, in the pages ahead we invite you to join us in reflecting on God's relational revolution that is underway!

Dear Reader,

At some point in our lives, we all encounter a difficulty or a challenge that causes us to question everything we have ever known. If we steward that pain well, we eventually enter into what Richard Rohr calls the "second half of life."[1]

This "second half of life" involves knowing the rules but realizing we no longer see them in the same light. It becomes clear that rules alone are not enough to bring about character change and healthy relationships. Something more is needed.

Each of us—John, Kent and Toni–have been searching for that "more" ever since we hit our own existential crises: be it a failing marriage, a child who could not be helped, or a ministry that was burning people out and leaving pain in its wake. The second half of life came calling to us with an invitation to a radical relational pursuit, and we have been growing into that new way of being ever since.

We are part of an organization called Luke 10, or LK10 for short. We are a community of "second-half-of-lifers,"

[1] *Falling Upward: A Spirituality for the Two Halves of Life*

maturing elders and trainers who are learning from one another as we explore uncharted relational territory in the Body of Christ.

LK10 has a place for “first-half-of-lifers” as well. Life inevitably brings crises. *Before* disorientation hits is the time to learn the critical relational skills that will build resilience to not only survive but thrive in the years to come. It is also comforting and empowering to be in a community with folks who understand what you are going through because they have already navigated similar difficulties in life.

Training for this “relational revolution” is only possible because of the donations and gifts of generous patrons, and we thank you. Because the proceeds of this book go to funding LK10, every reader makes a difference! Every purchase enables a maturing spiritual mom and dad to rediscover their calling and enter into a relational way of leading their families, churches, and communities. You are helping create a vibrant family of Jesus within reach of every person on the planet!

We hold you in our hearts as you journey through these pages in search of “more.” May your heart find the words to express what you sense stirring. And may you find companions to journey with you along the way.

The Authors

What Is God Doing?

Are you experiencing it?

An amazing spiritual and relational revolution is currently underway. The Bride of Christ is returning to her original love. God is renewing, redefining, and reconstructing her into the life-receiving, life-giving community she was designed to be.

God's invitation to vibrant, beloved community is breaking into our way of life. God is telling a story that demands disruption, reclaiming a relational Christian culture for our time that reveals the multifaceted wisdom of the God who is love.[2]

An amazing spiritual and relational revolution is currently underway.

This story calls us deeper into joy-fueled relationship. It can be summed up in three phrases:

[2] Eph. 3:10-11

> In the beginning was Joy.
> In the end will be deeper Joy.
> In between is an astounding invitation: "Come share our joy!"

Two scenes bookend our place in this narrative.

> Before God said, "Let us make humankind in our image;"
> Before God planted the "garden of joy;"
> Before the eternal Word spoke;
> Before the Spirit brooded over the watery chaos;
> There was Father, Son, and Spirit: an amazing communion, a gift-giving community, an interdependent family of love sharing life in an eternal dance of joy.

At the end of the story, we find the fellowship of delight. The Father is present; the Son is present; the Spirit is present. But there is another present—she, along with the Spirit, invites the reader to "Come!"

The Spirit and the bride say, "Come." And let the one who hears say, "Come." And let the one who is thirsty come; let the one who desires, take the water of life without cost.[3]

Beckoning the hearer is the beautiful Bride of Christ—the Church—a diverse multitude of humans descended from the original family bearing the divine image in every language, tribe, and people.[4] The bride bears God's

[3] Revelation 22:17
[4] Rev. 7:9-10

regenerative life. She is the companion made for the ever-expanding celebration of the God who is love. An invitation to deeper joy is before us as the "still, small voice" of God beckons us,[5] "Come and share in our delight."

Throughout history, this invitation has become hidden or distorted by the imperfect cultures that God's people have formed. In His love and grace, God breaks in and stirs our hearts to desire more of Him and more of each other. A longing is kindled, and we again hear the call: "Come!"

In each church renewal throughout history, when God's people heeded our hunger and answered that call, we realized that God's story is an invitation to something much greater than our current Christian experience. So much more.

In our day, God's true, interdependent, intergenerational, joy-filled life is again whispering, "Come!" And in this call, God invites us, his people, out of a distorted identity that is no longer good news to the world. God offers us a radical experience of salvation and church, one that brings life and good news to all because it returns healthy relationship to the center of all we are.[6]

While God's invitation disrupts the current state of the church, the Spirit of God is raising various groups and

---

[5] 1 Kings 19:12

[6] For evidence of a distorted, weakened, harmful prevalent church culture see *Escaping Enemy Mode* by Dr. Jim Wilder and Ray Woolridge. Or listen to the podcast "The Rise and Fall of Mars Hill."

communities with a fresh vision for a church that *is* good news. Several of these organizations are networking with each other, learning together, and living a new relationship-based culture that bears hope for many worldwide.[7]

Who We Are

We are Luke 10 (LK10), a network of joy-fueled, Jesus-led, communities of practice. We hail from over 39 countries and number in the thousands, sharing connections with like-minded Christian families and organizations throughout the world. We were founded in 2008 as a result of decades of John White and Kent Smith exploring what would need to shift in Christian culture for the people of God to become a vibrant expression of God's hands and feet here on earth. Their experience starting churches, leading churches, and training church leaders revealed that revolutionary change was needed in Western Christian culture.

During these years, God was raising up other organizations with the purpose of helping Christians return to a relational understanding of faith. Toni Daniels, a church planter in South America, had trained with several of these other organizations.[8] Her passion to be church in a way that nurtures people's relational health led her to LK10 in 2014.

---

[7] See "Additional Resources" after the last chapter for a list of organizations who are training others in living out the values found in this book.

[8] Toni had received training from relationally based organizations such as Godly Play, Life Model Works, THRIVEToday, as well as The Immanuel Approach.

She has had a key role in taking LK10's equipping to new levels of effectiveness in what was by then a growing, worldwide movement.

LK10 is hard to visualize. We cannot be defined by where we meet or what structure of church we look like. We are not limited by a person, a program, a denomination, a form of church or a building. We meet in large gatherings, small groups, and micro-expressions. We encounter Christ-community in church buildings, homes, community centers, hospitals, and businesses, over coffee, and online.

We are more defined by a set of values we embody. Values that move us into practicing church in ways that express the fullness of God's life–a fullness revealed when the whole community is vibrant and empowered, loving one another as well as those who are different.

Our vision is to see vibrant families of Jesus in close reach of everyone on the planet. We see this as God's vision for the consummation of history: everything aligned under the lordship of Jesus.

Our mission is to connect and equip maturing spiritual parents (leaders) who can nurture this revolution–this culture of God's arriving Kingdom.

We are just one of these tribes heralding the shift towards a relational view of salvation and church. We are networking with others as we train communities of men and women, church planters, missionaries, pastors, and seminary professors–spiritual leaders who embrace the relational revolution that is underway.

We are a Christian movement fueled by joy and led by Jesus: spiritual moms and dads all over the world training together to spontaneously love everyone. And thousands are learning to nurture beloved communities that represent the multifaceted wisdom of God to the world.

The book before you declares the values of this revolution, supported by our combined knowledge and experience, and that of other groups with which we are associated. It also reveals how these values revolutionize an ineffective and, at times, harmful Christian culture.

Out of these values, God's people experience and offer a way of *being* church rather than simply *doing* church. God is drawing people back to the original intent of church: healthily connected family,[9] not merely a program, organization, or institution.

This book is *not* a comprehensive treatment of the five values and the cultural shifts they represent. It is meant to be more of a declaration than a thorough explanation. It is written in a language of vision, outlining broad concepts with enough specificity to convey the idea. Those seeking a more detailed outline will be pleased to know that in

---

[9] Mark 10:29-31, Roger Gehring commenting on 1 Tim. 3:15 in *Houses Church and Mission: The Importance of Household. Structures in Early Christianity*: "...'house or family of God' becomes…the central, all-guiding image for the self-understanding and organization of the church." p. 261

addition to our book *Joy Fueled*, four more books will be published soon that will explore each core value in detail. These will outline our teaching at a level suitable for implementation.[10]

A Clarion Call

There is a cry for healthy relationships within the Body of Christ. While slowly building for centuries, the cry is now so widespread that it can no longer be ignored. Over 65 million people have walked away from institutional church in the United States alone–many to "save their faith." That is astonishing![11] While these stats are specific to the US, we have observed a similar phenomenon in dozens of nations worldwide as people reach out to connect and train with others in this relational revolution.

As Christian leaders, we must pay attention to why people are leaving and to hear what God wants to release into his bride today–not to tear down the church but rather help her become all she was created to be.

We are not saying large Christian gatherings are bad or wrong; or that house church or some version of "simple church" is the answer. We are drawn to something much deeper than the outward shape of our meetings. We are

---

[10] Go to LK10.com/bookupdate to be added to the notification list when published.

[11] *Exodus of the Religious Dones*: Research revealing the size, make-up, and motivations of the formerly churched population.

focused on culture. This includes our values and practices that are lived out as our stories intersect.

Understanding the dynamics of culture can help us see how we have been shaped by both healthy and unhealthy values and practices. Identifying the values that define us as we answer the call to "Come!" is the first step. This is what we hope to bring in the pages that follow. Based on those value shifts come corresponding changes in our practices and in how we live and love together.

So many want a how-to book. However, simply tweaking practices and meetings is not enough, for as you will see, the problem goes much deeper to the core of how we define ourselves as the people of God or the church. Defining ourselves primarily by what we believe and do has proven ineffective, divisive and even harmful. Christian character, as defined by Dallas Willard and Dr. Jim Wilder, is the ability to spontaneously love those around us, even our enemies. This level of character change is not achieved by beliefs or willful choice alone.[12]

This does not mean we do not have beliefs or exercise our will, but that we recognize that our intimate connections are what lead us. And as such, we must move healthy attachment and relational connection to the center of our Christian practices, where our true heart resides. That is

---

[12] For a full treatment of how ineffective intellectual belief and will are at producing Christian character see *Renovated: God, Dallas Willard and the Church That Transforms* by Dr. Jim Wilder.

how we access the new heart we have been given in Christ.[13]

The will and intellectual beliefs must be subordinated to a secondary place. They remain important, but what defines us is primarily *who* we love and who loves us, and secondarily *what* we love.

God invites us to identify ourselves by who we love. Instead of merely *thinking about* God, the call to "Come!" is an invitation to love and be loved, to enter an interactive, stable connection with our fellow humans and the God of the universe–one who gives us a new heart able to spontaneously love even those who believe differently than we do.

Imagine what it would look like to be identified as "those who walk with God; people whose lifestyle is love."

For us, shifting to a culture centered on healthy connection with God and others has meant letting go of our settled certainties about how things must be, and instead, following Jesus into every dimension of life together. This departure from the familiar has been intensely challenging, out of control, disorienting, and yet incredibly freeing and life-giving.

Why is this transformation crucial? Because the good news that God offers the world is not merely a set of beliefs, a creed, or a ticket to heaven, but God himself. God is the

---

[13] Ezekiel 11:19

one and only, dwelling here and now in a collective people embodying a new culture–a *kingdom* culture. "Your kingdom come, your will be done, on earth as it is in heaven."[14]

We do not have the luxury of sliding easily into new kingdom values and practices. Neither did the disciples. We have the onerous process of unlearning our present culture and entering into a relationship beyond our control. This is an intentional, internal, and collective work. It requires a local focus beginning with our immediate family culture: the spirit which inhabits our very homes.

To experience for ourselves and offer the good news of relational wholeness when our inherited versions of church are losing the hearts of millions, we need to reconstruct that very culture. We need to accept God's challenging call to listen for new practices that lead us into joy and deeper heart connection with God and others.

But, of course, Jesus knew this from the start:

Whoever wants to save their own life will lose it, but whoever loses their life for me and my good news will save it.[15]

The people of God today need to be willing to "lose" the cultural life they know in order to experience the full salvation Jesus offers. While this work is not easy, and may even seem scary for those just starting out in life, mature

---

[14] Mattthew 6:10
[15] Mark 8:35

men and women are leading the process for those who are still maturing into spiritual adulthood. We are among them.

Maybe you are among us?

If so, we invite you to "Come! Share in Our delight."

1

The "Dones"

In case you're just now hearing of the mass church exodus and the participatory revolution, we want to catch you up with what church researchers have observed over the last twenty years.

The church used to ask, "How can we change the world's culture?" The question now is: "How can we change the church's culture so that it is once again good news of salvation for the world?"

In 2005, George Barna, a well-known church researcher, declared in his book, *Revolution,* that there was "an explosion of spiritual energy and activity" happening that was "an unprecedented re-engineering of America's faith dimension that is likely to be the most significant transition in the religious landscape that you will ever experience." "This Revolution," he continued, "is on track to become the most significant recalibration of the American Christian body in more than a century."[16]

[16] Barna, *Revolution*, p. ix.

Notice those words…*re-engineering*, *recalibration*. Eighteen years ago, Barna could see the beginnings of God re-engineering or recalibrating his church.

The church used to ask, "How can we change the world's culture?" The question now is: "How can we change the church's culture so that it is once again good news of salvation for the world?"

At the same time as Barna's book was published, Reggie McNeal, a Southern Baptist church consultant, noticed the same God-movement happening. He wrote in *The Present Future* that "the current church culture in North America is on life support…. The imminent demise under discussion is the collapse of the unique culture in North America that has come to be called church… A growing number of people are leaving the institutional church for a new reason. They are not leaving because they have lost faith. They are leaving to preserve their faith."[17]

This is worth repeating. In 2005 (eighteen years before publishing this book), people were leaving the church to *preserve* their faith! That exodus has only continued to grow over the years.

[17] McNeal, *The Present Future*. p, 1, 4.

When the books by Barna and McNeal came out, many church leaders felt their messages were extreme, even alarmist. However, it turns out that the revolution these authors saw coming was actually deeper and broader than imagined.

Ten years later, in 2015, sociologist Josh Packard published the results of a quantitative study documenting this mass church exodus–how many had left the church and what their motivations were for leaving.[18] Packard quantified the demise that McNeal saw coming. He showed it was no longer imminent; it was actually happening!

Packard reported that “the data from the national survey reveal that 31 percent of American adults (65 million people) who were once regular church attenders have opted out of organized religion altogether. Roughly half of these people, or 30.5 million U.S. adults, still express a Christian identity.” He called these people “the Dones.” They were once part of a church, often as pastors or leaders, but had now left and weren’t going back. They were done.

Packard’s research agreed with McNeal’s assessment that, “many see leaving the church as the only way to save their faith.”[19] Those leaving the institutional form of church expressed a desire for community life that was not centrally organized by a large institution. Packard explained that these people were not necessarily angry; they simply found

---

[18]*Exodus of the Religious Dones*: Research revealing the size, make-up, and motivations of the formerly churched population.
[19] *Church Refugees: Sociologists Reveal Why People Are DONE With Church But Not Their Faith*

that churches were ill-equipped to bring about true transformation leading to vibrant lives.

Packard also found an additional 7 million "Almost Dones." These people still attended an institutional church but were thinking seriously about leaving.

The present revolution is massive.

In 2019, sensing this church exodus gaining momentum, a group of 50 evangelical scholars, institutional pastors, and church leaders met at Wheaton College to consider the state of the church in America.[20] Among them were Tim Keller, Presbyterian mega-church pastor, and Mark Labberton, President of Fuller Seminary.

Here's the stunning conclusion that these *mainstream evangelical leaders* came to:

"The pastor-led, program-centric, building/facility-based church that is so predominant in the US today is the church that is positioned to die. We have effectively been starting Blockbuster video stores in 2019. No one is coming."[21]

---

[20] This think tank was hosted by the Send Institute which is a ministry of the Billy Graham Center at Wheaton college. Two members of the think tank reported on the findings of that gathering in a podcast. That podcast ("State of the Church in America", Episode 25) can be accessed here: https://ephesiology.com/2019/10/22/ep-25-ephesiologists-at-the-send-institute/.

[21] This statement was made by *institutional church pastors* and leaders, not by church planting revolutionaries. If you are a pastor who has been working on your emotional health and leading more

And that diagnosis was before COVID-19 hit hard in 2020. According to the Barna Group, one in three practicing Christians dropped out of church completely during COVID, and many churches closed permanently.[22]

Note these church leaders are not saying church buildings are bad or that every church building will close its doors. Rather, a Christian culture centered around the pastor, the program and/or the building is a culture that is *positioned* to die. Meanwhile, the Body of Christ hears the whisper "Come!" and its members are longing for more.

While many pastors of conventional churches want to shift Christian practices to be more participatory and relational, the task often seems impossible. It's as if they are swimming upstream alone.

The relational revolution is complex with various expressions. While the values shared herein can be implemented in the context of a traditional church setting or even a family setting, they may be met with great challenge. A community of like-minded leaders is highly recommended as you follow God in training to receive and give love more consistently.

---

effectively than ever, you are one of the few who are fighting against the current of an unhealthy Christian culture that is undermining your hard work. We don't mean to discourage you or invalidate all the good you are bringing to your congregation. We want to identify what makes your work so hard and what is causing so many to walk away. We want to create a new culture together.

[22] https://ifstudies.org/blog/the-decline-in-church-attendance-in-covid-america

The first-century church was centered on a healthy attachment with God and with each other; it was relationally based. Jesus spent three years living with his disciples, delighting in them, modeling and teaching among other things an interactive connection with God. He was re-training them on how to love each other, even those who opposed them.

Millions of Christians long for a healthy, integrated Christian community that walks with God.

While a seismic change like this is difficult, disruptive, and deeply distressing for many, it also opens the space for new hope and possibility. The facts are these:

- God is the initiator of this revolution.
- God is at work in these seismic shifts in Christian culture.
- God is drawing his people back to his original intent for the church.

What would a church that is healthily connected to God and each other look like? How can a church nurture strong relational attachment with God and each other as the primary means for changing people's beliefs and behaviors?

This relational revolution is a movement of believers who are:

Joy-Fueled
Jesus-led
Communities of Practice, training as
Spiritual Parents, in order to nurture
Ecosystems of Grace.

These are the values the church needs. This is who you are invited to become. We will not only break them down in the following chapters, but we will also share what changes these Christian cultural shifts require. Letting go and unlearning has to happen in order to follow Jesus as you answer God's call to "Come! Share in Our delight." Therein is great delight!

2

Joy Fueled

Declaration 1

As we follow God's lead, we leave behind guilt and shame as primary motivators. We see salvation as healthy, joyful connection to God. Consequently, we encounter church as a joy-based relationship with each other and God. We are not guilt-ridden nor duty-driven. We have found that it is "his kindness that leads to repentance."[23]

God is glad to be with us no matter what. We can be fueled by the most powerful force alive: joy.

God loves. In fact, "God is love,"[24] and where love is being expressed and received, the joy of God is also flowing. Joy is primarily relational, be it a relationship with God, with another human, or even with yourself! It can also be experienced in memories of joyful moments together, in gift exchanging, and acts of service. We primarily feel joy when someone enjoys us, delights in who we are, and

---

[23] Romans 2:4

[24] 1 John 4:8

wants to be with us, no matter what we are feeling in the moment, and no matter what we have done in the past. We are precious to them, and they show it on their face or through their actions.

Joy flows from giving and receiving love—which is the life of God. Nothing brings us closer to the center of all creative power than the joy of God expressed in the face of Christ and each other. "For the joy set before Him, He endured the cross."[25] Christ was so delighted by the image of being united with us that he endured torture and death to fully be with us.

Joy flows from giving and receiving love —which is the life of God.

We now know through studies in neuro-science that this pattern of love-sparking-joy forms the basis from earliest infancy for all healthy human development.[26] When we see a baby light up in the presence of her smiling mother, we're witnessing the genesis of joy fuel being formed in another life. This is love embodied—God's life.

The Greek language of the New Testament offers intriguing insight. The words for joy, gift and gratitude are

---

[25] Hebrews 12:2

[26] *The Life Model: Living From the Heart Jesus Gave You* by Dr. James G Friesen, Dr E. James Wilder, Anne M. Bierling, Rick Koepcke and Maribeth Poole

closely related. All share the same root, char—pronounced "car." Here's the connection:

- Joy—Chara (delight)
- Gift or Grace—Charis (that which brings joy or delight)
- Gratitude—Eucharistia (joy or delight returned)

These three ideas together, in any language, describe what love-in-action looks like. Lovers give a gift to show their delight in the one they love. On receiving the gift, joy wells up in the beloved. Naturally, they say "thank you!" and deeper joy flows back to the lover.

Love grows in the dance of joy between gift and gratitude. More love, more joy. This is astounding. What other process do we know that, all by itself, produces more than it starts with?

Love-ignited joy is the one perpetual-motion fuel. Nothing else compares.

Love grows in the dance of joy between gift and gratitude. More love, more joy.

This joy flows from giving and receiving delight and taps into God's own life—the most enduring, powerful and motivational fuel of all.[27] Instead of living out of shame, guilt or duty, we experience a deep sense of joy that makes the relationship greater than any problems we face.

The Cultural Shift

Christian culture has often been characterized by a limited and ultimately harmful fuel source that many of us have used at some point in our lives: the gospel of knowledge and duty. This way of thinking says that if we just get more knowledge and try harder, we will grow, mature, feel satisfied, and want to serve God and others. There is little attention to love or relational bonding; it is all about intellect and will. When knowledge and duty are all we have, they are not really good news (the meaning of gospel) because, as Galatians 3:21-22 tells us, in the long run, this knowledge and duty cannot produce righteousness. Only a secure connection with God can do that.[28]

Knowledge and duty produce guilt and obligation, which can be effective at starting an engine but, unfortunately, this fuel, so to speak, corrodes over time, competes with joy, and eventually smothers it out altogether.

Being Joy-fueled, on the other hand, means you know that even when you cannot "do" anything for God today, God loves you and deeply enjoys being with you, anyway. God is not in a relationship with you just to use you; he actually

---

[27] John 15:11

[28] For a complete treatment of salvation as secure attachment to God see *Renovated: God, Dallas Willard, and the Church that Transforms* by Dr. Jim Wilder

loves and delights in just being with you. He is interested in your feelings and emotions.

Unfortunately, Christian culture taught us that if we trust God, we will not be overwhelmed with fear, anger, sadness, shame, or hopeless despair. We, as Christians,

---

God is not in a relationship with you just to use you; he actually loves and delights in just being with you. He is interested in your feelings and emotions.

---

have been encouraged to ignore our feelings and choose "faith" instead. This has done unimaginable damage to the Body of Christ. Trusting is a process that begins with acknowledging present reality. As long as we deny our genuine emotions (thinking we are not supposed to feel them), we are defeated before we begin. Relationship is based on honesty and heart-to-heart connection. When we ignore our feelings, we are living a lie.

The reality is that when we deny our emotions–especially the difficult ones–they do not go away! Instead, they are allowed to sabotage us by influencing our reactions, trapping us in isolation and pain, even though we may be completely unaware of them.

When we look to the Bible for wisdom, we find a book filled with emotion! The Psalms give us guidance on what to do with our heavier feelings. David modeled brutal honesty with himself and God as he wrote out his feelings in songs or poems. Some people call his heavier works "Psalms of Disorientation," because David seems confused as he tries to understand how his feelings can be integrated with the truth about himself and God.[29]

The Christian life is not about denying our feelings but about receiving this all-encompassing love, this delight in the midst of our hard feelings until the joy wells up and overflows. Leading out of joy means we do not have to over-commit ourselves in order to feel loved or accepted. It means we can take time to receive until we can give out of the abundance within us.

Jesus says it this way in Matthew 11:28-29 MSG:

Are you tired? Worn out? Burned out on religion? Come to me. Get away with me and you'll recover your life. I'll show you how to take a real rest. Walk with me and work with me—watch how I do it. Learn the unforced rhythms of grace. I won't lay anything heavy or ill-fitting on you. Keep company with me and you'll learn to live freely and lightly.

God is calling His people out of the gospel of knowledge and duty and into something much more intimate and heart-centered. He is inviting us into the "unforced rhythms" of grace that flow from a healthy relationship with God. The word *unforced* is particularly important.

---

[29] Examples of Psalms of Disorientation: Ps. 13, Ps 35, Ps 74, Ps 79, Ps 88, Ps 109. Especially Ps 22 which Jesus himself prayed while on the cross in Mt 27:46.

This is what it means to be joy fueled. Instead of forcing ourselves to do and be, we admit our weakness, our exhaustion, our true feelings, and we let Jesus (and others) meet us there, hold us, invite us into joy and pull us through.

Paying attention to the heart is essential in this process. Unconditional acceptance means we create safe spaces to share our emotions and feelings in helpful ways that do not overwhelm others. We are known and loved in our weaknesses. And that brings good news that wells up inside of us and motivates us.

This is a radical departure from the ways we have often been motivated by church culture in the past. In the same way, this statement Jesus made in Matthew was a radical departure for the Jewish leaders 2,000 years ago.

Unconditional acceptance means we create safe spaces to share our emotions and feelings in helpful ways that do not overwhelm others.

As we follow God's lead, we leave behind guilt and shame as primary motivators. We see salvation as healthy, joyful connection to God. Consequently, we encounter church as a joy-based relationship with each other and God. Of course, this takes practice to cultivate. That time is valuable; healthy, heart-to-heart connection cannot be short-circuited.

Are you done living the Christian life as only a list of intellectual beliefs and duties? Do you want a vibrant relationship that changes you from the inside out? Do you want to experience that promise in Jeremiah 31 that was fulfilled at Pentecost and repeated in Hebrews 8:10-12:

"This is the covenant I will establish with the people of Israel
after that time," declares the Lord.
"I will put my laws in their minds
and write them on their hearts.
I will be their God,
and they will be my people.
No longer will they teach their neighbor,
or say to one another, 'Know the Lord,'
because they will all know me,
from the least of them to the greatest.
For I will forgive their wickedness
and will remember their sins no more."

This is the good news. Let's embrace all that God has promised. Let's receive God's love and let God enjoy us so deeply that it radically changes our identity. Yes, this requires an interactive, consistent connection with God, which most of us were never taught to cultivate in our own church traditions. So, what does it look like for us to give up clinging to our intellect and let Jesus lead us?

Let's find out together.

3

Jesus Led

Declaration 2

We have renounced trusting in only our own ability to discern right from wrong or good from bad. We do not rely merely on principles or teachings or doctrines. We are committed to listening individually and together to the constant, ever-accessible presence of God who longs to love us, hold us, comfort us, challenge us, reveal our hearts, and lead us into all joy, peace, and truth.

The God who loves is a God who reveals because to love is to share. Throughout scripture, God speaks, God discloses. "And God said...,"[30] is a recurring refrain because self-expression is the fundamental gift a lover has to offer one who is loved. Revelation is the seed of God's loving initiative that awakens and invites the grateful love and participation of the beloved.

It's no surprise, then, that in the teachings of Jesus, the seed is the Word of God, where the in-breaking reign of God gets underway in human hearts. For Jesus, this was not just an abstract claim about the nature of God. Rather, it was

[30] Gen. 1:3, 6 ,9 ,11, 14, 20, 22, 24, 26, 28, 29

the dominant reality that shaped his daily life: "I do nothing of my own initiative but only speak what the Father has revealed to me."[31] Not only did the Father tell him what to say, he also told him how to say it.[32]

Jesus said the same was true for us–his followers; "My sheep are continually hearing my voice."[33] In this verse, the form of the verb "to hear" is particularly important. The present tense implies continuous action. "Continually hearing" is the key phrase. In other words, God desires an ongoing intimate conversational relationship with us.

The *Living Word*–Jesus–is still speaking today. While sensing God's voice has been abused over the lifetime of the church, we can no longer let fear of getting it wrong allow Christian culture to dismiss the relational nature of God. At the same time, we continue to measure what we hear. We test what we hear with scripture and with our community.

The God of the Bible has always had and continues to have an infinite palette of revelational tools. Think: dreams, burning bushes, talking donkeys, handwriting on walls, still, small voices in deep caves.

God wants to connect with us in real-time through images, sensations, feelings, thoughts, scriptures, songs, etc., to

---

[31] John 8:28
[32] John 12:49-50
[33] John 10:27

comfort, guide and empower us so we "overflow with hope by the power of the Holy Spirit."[34]

Being Jesus-led is about thinking *with* God, not just *about* God. It is about growing a steady, consistent relational connection with God and others, instead of merely reading about God or only occasionally sensing God.

God wants to connect with us in real-time through images, sensations, feelings, thoughts, scriptures, songs, etc., to comfort, guide and empower us so we "overflow with hope by the power of the Holy Spirit."

As the writer to the Hebrews repeatedly reminds us, "Oh, that today you would listen as God speaks! Do not harden your hearts…."[35] God's life, grace, and truth are available to us fresh each day if we are ready to receive them. We have not been left to figure out life on our own. Rather we have been given a counselor–the Holy Spirit who guides us together day by day.[36]

[34] Romans 15:13
[35] Hebrews 3:7,15
[36] John 14:15-17, 16:5-15

The Cultural Shift

While many churches claim to be Jesus-led, the Christian culture many people experience holds to a worldview that elevates intellectual knowledge and understanding of Biblical truth over an interactive relationship with God. This focus results in functionally living as though God were not actually with us at all.

This is exactly the problem Jesus had with the Jews in his day. He told them, "You diligently study the scriptures because you think that by them you possess eternal life. These are the scriptures that testify about me yet you refuse to come to me to have life."[37] These Jews were the best Bible scholars of their day but they totally missed a relationship with Jesus.

While many churches claim to be Jesus-led, the Christian culture many people experience holds to a worldview that elevates intellectual knowledge and understanding of Biblical truth over an interactive relationship with God.

This type of predominantly left-brained Christianity, still common today, promotes the idea that most people cannot really hear God speak. Maybe a few people like the pastor

[37] John 5:39

and the elders/leaders can hear from God, but normal people cannot, and it would be dangerous if they could!

Therefore, as this mindset goes, the best we can do is to adhere to the principles the Bible teaches. So, we study principles as if our life depends on it and excessively focus on teaching them to others. The thought is that if people just knew the right things to do and how to think, they would make better choices. That seems much safer and easier than actually training people to listen and relate to a living God.

We are left with a WWJD Christianity–trying to guess in any given situation, "What Would Jesus Do?" In this way of thinking, we do *not* live as if Jesus is right here, right now. In this culture, our ability to follow God comes down to having enough of the right information to calculate the truth on our own.

However, we will *never* have enough right information to navigate life on our own. "On our own" is not how we are designed to navigate life.

Unfortunately, those of us raised in Christian homes, who learned so much of the Bible and Christian culture all of our lives, are the ones who have had an even harder time relying on Jesus instead of primarily our own knowledge. Our self-created Christian identities seem so "right" to us, just as Paul's passion to kill Christians seemed so "right" to him. It has taken experiencing very difficult life circumstances like divorce, mental illness, ministry burn-out, and family fall-out to bring many of us to the place where we are ready to let go of all we thought we knew to be "right," and to radically cultivate a relationship with God where we sense his presence and begin to trust his thoughts about good and bad, right and wrong, instead of our own.

In addition, good information alone does not seem to be working very well in achieving true character change. If it were effective, then our Christian leaders (who have the most training to understand the Bible) would be the last people to engage in affairs, abuse of staff and family, and addiction. In reality, more information alone seems to leave these leaders just as susceptible to moral failure as those who know nothing of God's Word.[38]

Where current Christian culture has promoted listening to God, often it has done so only as an individual encounter rather than a normal, daily, communal endeavor. But individual encounter, while beneficial, cannot reveal the multifaceted wisdom of God. For that, we need each other.

Overall, most Christians do not know how to sense God's presence, and current discipleship training does not typically involve equipping people to healthily connect with the presence of God with their individual and collective imagination.

Though we as God's people have longed for supernatural power and wisdom, we, unfortunately, have all too often

---

[38] Again, see *Renovated: God, Dallas Willard and the Church that Transforms* by Dr. Jim Wilder.

depended on our own human effort. In this culture, heart-to-heart connection is replaced with service and study, duty and obligation, success and image. Such Christian culture has often become the perfect breeding ground for Functional Deism, where we believe God exists, but we function as if he is distant and uncommunicative; the exact opposite of love being expressed and received.

How did we get here? It's a long story, but a key change occurred when the Enlightenment of the 1700s focused on head knowledge over relationship, producing a philosophical shift from which Christian culture has never fully recovered. This shift created a skewed paradigm that has left the church offering solutions for character change that have not worked.[39]

In this culture, heart-to-heart connection is replaced with service and study, duty and obligation, success and image. Such Christian culture has often become the perfect breeding ground for Functional Deism.

This diseased culture has gone on long enough. The people of God are longing for a healthy emotional, spiritual connection with Immanuel, "God with us," where we sense God's voice individually and together. God is drawing us

[39] See E. James Wilder and Marcus Warner, *The Solution of Choice: Four Good Ideas That Neutralized Western Christianity*, 2018.

back to a secure relationship with the God of beloved community where love can again grow in the dance of joy between gift and gratitude.

If Father, Son, and Spirit are ever-present and actively revealing themselves to us,[40] then we can live in constant communion with the life of God that is being poured out to us as individuals, families, and communities. We have not been left alone with only a written guide to follow.

The relational revolution underway is based on an ongoing, healthy, emotional connection with God, not what we think we know about God. Being able to experience God in real-time, here and now, allows us to be truly led by the joy, peace, and power that emanates from the life of the Trinity!

The question remains, "How do we become a people that can clearly and consistently discern God's presence and guidance among us?"

The answer: We practice together.

How do we become a people that can clearly and consistently discern God's presence and guidance among us? We practice together.

---

[40] Mt. 3:16-17, John 14:15-17, John 16:12-15, John 17:20-23, Mt. 28:19, 2 Cor. 13:14

4

Communities of Practice

Declaration 3

We are communities of practice living into the alternative story God is telling. One of joy, peace, and hope. We realize that loving well takes practice, especially because we want to grow to spontaneously love others, even those who disagree with us or oppose us. That is how the world will know we are God's people, by this alternative story of spontaneously loving each other well.[41] *We have experienced the power of practicing together in communities with others who are growing and learning to love, and we are committed for life.*

Austrian philosopher and Roman Catholic priest, Ivan Illich, once said,

> Neither revolution nor reformation can ultimately change a society, rather you must tell a new powerful tale, one so persuasive that it sweeps away the old myths and becomes the preferred

[41] John 13:35

> story, one so inclusive that it gathers all the bits of our past and our present into a coherent whole, one that even shines some light into the future so that we can take the next step… If you want to change a society, then you have to tell an alternative story.

God is telling an alternative story—a life that is joy fueled and Jesus led. A story of loving and being loved, of giving and receiving.

To live into the counter-story God is telling we must unlearn some automatic negative ways we relate to each other and learn new skills that create intimacy, resiliency and belonging. Relational skills grow just like physical skills; we learn to play an instrument or a sport or even speak a new language the same way we learn how to form healthy relationships. We long for the skills of loving to become part of our involuntary function, where we automatically respond in kind ways before we even have a chance to think about what "kind" would look like. Many have only begun to learn this kingdom culture by practicing joy, quiet, appreciation, and listening to God together in the context of our stories.

God is telling an alternative story—a life that is joy fueled and Jesus led. A story of loving and being loved, of giving and receiving.

Isn't this how Jesus did it? Jesus began his revolution by calling together a small group of people to be with him, to give and receive together in mutually satisfying, devoted relationships. This small band of brothers and sisters were witnessing and *practicing* the life of God's love–the good news–*together*. This was not a community of *perfection,* but a community of *practice*, one where the disciples were allowed to get it wrong, receive feedback, and try again.

This new culture includes cultivating skills such as joy, quieting, curiosity, sensing God's presence with us in real-time, and many more. We learn these skills, as well as our unique contribution, by practicing *in a community*, as the disciples did with Jesus. Overwhelming evidence shows that this is how people learn best.[42] And we can attest to that!

Organizations and institutions, including churches, are meant to be places where people can grow and mature through feedback and support. In this alternative story, we are experiencing church not only as healthy family but also as communities of practice.

Many of us have kicked against this idea of "practicing" loving. "Loving should be natural, and practicing together

---

[42] For example, in a ten year, 230-million-dollar study by the Eli Lilly Foundation, it was demonstrated that young adults were best formed in their Christian calling through coaching, apprenticeship and communities of practice. See Tim Clydesdale, *The Purposeful Graduate, 2015.*

feels so contrived," some say. The problem is that, in our experience, we have not learned to naturally love![43]

In the days when extended family was commonplace, life together with a diversity of people who knew us well was not only possible–it was the norm. In other places and earlier centuries, followers of Jesus shared life together as a cultural given—intergenerational eating, playing, working, and praying together as a matter of course day by day.

Those days are gone. The time when we could simply assume that nearly everyone has a community with whom to practice the life of love has passed. If we are to have a community of *practice*, it will be intentional, or not at all.

Acquiring any new skill takes time and practice. We must repeat the drill as close to daily as possible if we want skills to become automatic habits that constitute a lifestyle. Yes, skill practice can be boring, repetitive, and unnatural. It costs us time and attention, emotional and physical energy. The author of Hebrews understood this when he wrote: *No discipline (training) seems pleasant at the time, but painful. Later on, however, it produces a harvest of righteousness and peace for those who have been trained by it.*[44]

Once a relational skill has been learned and practiced, it comes naturally because it is part of who we are. We don't

---

[43] *Transforming Fellowship: 19 Brain Skills that Build Joyful Community* by Christ M. Coursey
[44] Hebrews 12:11

have to think about how to act lovingly because we are loving.

Long before we understood the neurobiology of habit formation, the apostle Paul saw the truth of this principle: "*train* yourself to be godly."[45]

This Greek verb *gumnazo* (from which we get words like *gymnasium* and *gymnastics*) means "to train with one's full effort, i.e., with complete physical, emotional force." Imagine an ancient Greek champion preparing for a sporting event. God has designed our bodies, including our brains, to train for an automatic response in life-giving ways to difficult situations. Dallas Willard described this training as the "way to become the kind of person who does, easily and routinely, what Jesus said—does it without having to think much about it."[46]

Training takes knowing what to practice and what to correct. Thankfully, our brains remain moldable all of our lives, and we can continue to not only learn new skills but with a good coach we can correct bad form.

The time to practice the skills we want is not in difficult situations when we are overwhelmed or flooding emotionally. No tennis player practices their serve during a match! There is too much pressure and no room for mistakes. Training requires mistakes. The match reveals how much we have or have not practiced. We will be sorely

---

[45] 1 Timothy 4:7

[46] Dallas Willard, *Renovation of the Heart: Putting On the Character of Christ,* p. 238.

disappointed if we expect to play well without consistent practice beforehand, focusing on the micro-skills for a good serve.

If we want to see a harvest of righteousness and peace, we must form communities of practice where mutual training can happen. Only by practicing with others can we develop the love-skills that *automatically* unleash God's hope in us so that it overflows into the world around us.

The Cultural Shift

God is calling us to stop seeing church as a spectator sport where people simply attend a service in a building or listen to a sermon on the internet. Answering the call to "Come!" means recognizing that these ways of doing church do not afford us opportunities to *practice* healthy relationship. We have to stop trying to form people by passively receiving information. That model is failing everywhere at an alarming rate. Bible teaching alone is not enough to instill spiritual formation. No matter how slick, polished or attention-grabbing our information delivery systems become, they simply cannot replace a community that intentionally practices relationship together.

We also have to say goodbye to letting "mission" drive us. Most of us have unintentionally harmed people because we had our eye on the "mission" instead of on loving each other well.

If we want to see a harvest of righteousness and peace, we must form communities of practice where mutual training can happen. Only by practicing with others can we develop the love-skills that automatically unleash God's hope in us so that it overflows into the world around us.

In the name of ministry and mission, many leaders have burned out or blown up. "The Rise and Fall of Mars Hill"[47] and "The Bodies Behind the Bus"[48] podcasts document many times over how we in Christian leadership have hurt others in the name of Christ.

God's vision for the Church—the *ekklesia* or the "called out ones,"—is skillful, family-like, heart-to-heart connections with each other and God, which embodies the life of God here on earth. This requires rethinking how we spend our time together so that we actually practice healthy relationships regularly. How well we listen to each other, argue with each other, and accept one another's differences depends on how well we practice together and learn from

[47] https://podcasts.apple.com/us/podcast/the-rise-and-fall-of-mars-hill/id1569401963
[48] https://podcasts.apple.com/us/podcast/bodies-behind-the-bus/id1601586078

our interactions. Becoming a vibrant family of Jesus requires lots of practice.

No one can practice loving God and others by themselves! Effective love-training requires that we train *with* others. The skills Christians are developing in the relational revolution are relational skills; therefore, a relationship is required to practice them–a healthily bonded, trusting relationship where people are allowed to make mistakes, accept feedback and try again. Ruptures in relationships are inevitable. Working to repair the connection is the path where these communities of practice forge intimacy and become anti-fragile.[49]

No one can practice loving God and others by themselves! Effective love-training requires that we train with others.

The new story of church we are living into, which is not new but ancient, is a vibrant family of Jesus–family meaning bonded by loving attachment, not merely by mission, biology or a set of beliefs. Living church healthily at this relational level requires the skills of connecting heart-to-heart with God and each other. These families need healthy spiritual moms and dads, those who may or

[49] Antifragility is a property of systems in which people increase in their capability to thrive as a result of stressors, shocks, volatility, noise, mistakes, faults, attacks, or failures. https://en.wikipedia.org/wiki/Antifragility

may not be biologically related, but who form healthy emotional bonds with others and nurture their emotional/spiritual growth.

When practicing listening, loving, giving, and receiving as closc to daily as possible, we as God's people become amazingly skilled at healthy connection. Like the best meaning of the word "parent," we are able to nurture or spiritually parent the communities around us. We become a non-anxious presence in the world, harvesting the fruit of the Spirit everywhere we go. We realize that what God invites us into is really so simple that children can understand and practice, and yet so profound that mastering it calls for a lifetime of learning.

Who is leading this relational revolution at the grassroots level?

Emotionally maturing spiritual parents.

5

Maturing Spiritual Parents

a.k.a. People of Peace

Declaration 4

We are a community made up of different generations including weak and strong alike. As older members of our society, we seek to sacrificially care for our children first and then once they are grown, we give our lives to sacrificially caring for our entire communities. We are "people of peace."[50] *We know this takes maturity, emotional and spiritual alike.*

We are among those maturing all over the world, whom God has prepared to help harvest his love, joy, peace, patience, kindness, goodness, gentleness and self-control. We do not have to overwork ourselves or care for communities outside of our ability. We get to be God's children, grow where we are weak, and overflow as we receive. We can call on God to send out more people of

---

[50] Matthew 10:11; Luke 10:6

peace and trust God to do so. As He does, we get to connect with them and mutually train one another.

In Luke 10, when Jesus sent out his disciples in pairs, he instructed them to keep their focus on one thing: finding "households of peace." In fact, he explicitly prohibited his disciples from focusing on anyone else. "Do not move around from house to house."[51] This seems strange, even counterintuitive. Why wouldn't Jesus have wanted his followers to reach everyone they could?

Jesus clearly had something in mind other than giving information about God to as many people as possible. His revolutionary strategy began in a different place–with the "Lord of the Harvest" who was at work in people and households before the disciples even arrived. [52]

Here's how Jesus says it:

Whenever you enter a house, first say, "May peace be on this house!" And if a person of peace is there, your peace will remain on him, but if not, it will return to you. Stay in that same house, eating and drinking what they give you, for the worker deserves his pay. Do not move around from house to house."[53]

The concept of a household or house of peace, *shalom bayit* in Hebrew, is well known in Jewish culture. In *Our Father Abraham, Jewish Roots of the Christian Faith*, Marvin

---

[51] Luke 10:7
[52] Luke 10:2
[53] Luke 10:4-7

Wilson writes, "...the Hebrew Bible often employs the word shalom in the sense of 'be in friendship, in right relations, in harmony' with others…A home of shalom, therefore, is a healthy home. Strife brings sickness but shalom is wellness and wholeness."[54]

In Luke 10, Jesus uses shalom to characterize both the household and the people living there. It was a home where God had already been at work establishing emotionally healthy relationships with each other and with those outside of the home.

It was likely that finding such a person and household provided the disciples with the context of a life-giving community. That family then could become a beachhead for the coming Kingdom of God through the trusting networks and secure relational connections already established. Clearly, Jesus was not just after converts–he was looking for people prepared to embody God's life, starting in their own homes.

Jesus' example teaches us that the shalom of God was preveniently at work in these homes before the disciples showed up on the scene.[55] As our understanding of Hebrew culture goes, even before they knew Christ, they were functioning as loving, emotionally healthy homes that brought peace to those around them. As a result of their healthy attachments, these people were already God-prepared, and the work of the disciples was relatively easy.

---

[54] P. 218

[55] Prevenient means "before."

Their job was to pay attention to which homes God was already at work in and share with them the good news of God's love through Christ. Cornelius in Acts 10 is a great example of this pre-work of God; because God had already been at work, Peter's role was not difficult.

Such people are formed over a lifetime in a maturation process designed by God that is fostered in healthy families from infancy through old age in all cultures. Neurothologian Jim Wilder and his associates have helpfully summarized this process as a growing capacity for nurture and love: from infant to child to adult to parent to elder.[56,57] When these families accept the call to share in God's delight, the good news spreads like a benevolent virus sweeping through the trusting relationships already established. Whole households come to faith, even whole communities. All because the healthy attachments were there to connect the dots.

In LK10, as we began to answer the call to "Come! Share in Our delight," we found others like us on the journey, "people of peace" that God had already prepared in advance to inaugurate a more relational culture of church. Within twelve years, leaders from thirty-nine countries found us because they were searching for more of what God has for them. We quickly realized we were not alone. We saw maturing people from all over the world answering God's call, each bringing their unique experience and

---

[56] https://lifemodelworks.org/jim-wilder/

[57] See James Wilder and others, *Living From the Heart Jesus Gave You,* 2013.

perspective. And we began to consistently call on God to send more laborers out into the field to harvest kingdom shalom.

In LK10, as we began to answer the call to "Come! Share in Our delight," we found others like us on the journey.

Unfortunately, many of us did not have the privilege of healthy family bonds that help us grow into families of peace. In communities of practice, we spiritual moms and dads (at the adult, parenting and eldering stages of maturity) train each other in the skills we missed growing up.[58] As we mature emotionally, we establish houses of peace where God's good news overflows in us and through us. We are able to love the younger and weaker in our midst and compassionately accompany them wherever they are in their stage of development.

Through this lens, we see Jesus functioning as a father with his disciples: "If you have seen me, you have seen the Father" and "I and the Father are one."[59] Jesus also spent three years with his disciples, which, according to developmental studies is approximately how long it would

---

[58] For a breakdown of the different stages of maturity see *The Life Model: Living From the Heart Jesus Gave You* by Friesen, Wilder, Koepcke, Bierling, Poole.
[59] Jn. 14:9; Jn. 10:30

have taken to "re-parent" them so that they inhabited the kingdom culture they were to pass on.[60]

Paul also understood and modeled the importance of spiritual parenting. To the Thessalonians, he wrote:

We were gentle among you, like a mother caring for her little children. We loved you so much that we were delighted to share with you not only the gospel of God but our lives as well, because you had become so dear to us...we dealt with each of you as a father deals with his own children, encouraging, comforting and urging you to live lives worthy of God, who calls you into his kingdom and glory.[61]

God is in the business of re-parenting us, inviting us into a life-giving family (the Trinity) and connecting us with brothers and sisters with whom we can train. We do not have to have all of the answers; we do not do all of the work. Christ commands us to "call on the Lord of the harvest to send out more workers."[62] It is our privilege to find each other, connect together, and train one another to continue to be "houses of peace" (spiritual parents) for those in need, not only in our own homes but in our

---

[60] See *The Life Model: Living From the Heart Jesus Gave You* by Friesen, Wilder, Koepcke, Bierling, Poole.
[61] 1 Thes. 2:7-8, 11-12
[62] Luke 10:2

extended families and beloved communities.[63]

The Cultural Shift

Becoming and training emotionally mature spiritual moms and dads is rarely ever a working concept in most current church systems. Intellectual maturity, gifting maturity, social maturity might be expected from leaders, however, none of these maturities actually ensure that we love one another. And sadly, spiritual maturity is often defined by how well we know Biblical principles, not how closely we sense God with us.

God is in the business of re-parenting us, inviting us into a life-giving family (the Trinity) and connecting us with brothers and sisters with whom we can train.

If we do not have emotional maturity then it will be increasingly hard to love those around us, especially those who disagree with us.

Often, what has characterized Christian culture is a system that promotes excellence (because if we look good, so does God) and is centered on mission (how many souls can be

[63] By "parent," we do not mean a position of authority or power assigned to someone, but a time-tested gentle protector who sacrificially cares for those around them.

saved) at the expense of receiving, resting, and relating healthily.

The values of the church system produce narcissistic leaders who are hired and empowered to "win" at all cost. And "winning" usually means growing church attendance and church impact. In these situations, staff meetings are combative and people are hurt yet shamed or fired if they speak up. Church departments compete for finances, and anyone who matures beyond the lead pastor is perceived as a threat and consequently let go.

This type of system encourages the followers to stay at child-level maturity because if they think for themselves, it could lead to divisions and other problems.

Often, what has characterized Christian culture is a system that promotes excellence (because if we look good, so does God) and is centered on mission (how many souls can be saved) at the expense of receiving, resting, and relating healthily.

The most devastating aspect of all, is that this culture of leadership promises a sense of family. However, instead of bonding for life, the relationship ends as soon as you no longer attend that church. These pseudo-family bonds were not strong enough to withstand people moving, changing jobs, or even disagreeing with each other. The problems always end up being larger than the relationships.

This culture produces and exploits highly gifted but emotionally immature communicators such as evangelists, teachers, and preachers who rely on their gifts to carry them forward. Unfortunately, this often means leaving a wake of destruction behind them because they (and those around them) lack the necessary emotional maturity or character needed to nurture healthy relational connections. Tragically, in some of our churches and denominations, even sexual abuse is ignored and hidden because it is believed that "the ends justify the means," and "the show must go on."[64]

While living out of this culture may fill an auditorium with hundreds or thousands, it primarily casts church as an audience, a business, or a machine. This view of church values giftedness and knowledge over character, and sees its leaders as CEOs, supervisors of "children," or even dictators who command and control instead of listen, nurture, and draw forth.

We have let go of these values and embraced participatory leadership. Healthy spiritual leaders draw forth the strength, beauty, and design of God in those around them, so they are never leading alone. Spiritual parenting at its

---

[64] https://www.christianitytoday.com/news/2019/february/southern-baptist-abuse-investigation-houston-chronicle-sbc.html

best is a relational endeavor where we accompany each person to become all God has made them to be. It is not a position of power that seeks to keep people powerless. Church grows at the speed of attachment, where heart-to-heart connection and character growth are more important than getting "results," whether increasing numbers, greater impact or silencing those who disagree with us.

The outcome of training as maturing spiritual moms and dads is a flourishing, extended family of people who are learning the practice of love. Even when our own story missed such a family, the new family that Jesus came to establish opens the way for us to discover our own relationship with God and the unfolding calling of God's love in our lives.

Healthy spiritual leaders draw forth the strength, beauty, and design of God in those around them, so they are never leading alone.

God is calling out the spiritual leaders in the world. While we may have different giftings, we are all called to love, care for, and nurture those around us. Jesus gave all leadership gifts to the church to draw out and equip all people to love.[65] A distinction in how people approach their

[65] Ephesians 4:11-13

loving can be based on their gifting, but not excluded because of their gifting.

We see God calling and networking his people globally, forming us into communities of practice to train in the relational skills necessary to nurture the coming awakening. We are not saying God is removing the leadership role of pastor (shepherd), nor are we saying every conventional church should sell its building.

We are saying God is correcting a Christian culture that *defines* church as a building, a business, or a spectator event centered on one person. We agree, it is time to be done with a Christian culture that breeds narcissists for senior leaders and passive spectators for members. Instead, we see all equipping leaders collaborating in a team to create spaces of *mutual* discipleship, where they learn to give and *receive* together. A church building may then become a training center where every member becomes a minister and every home becomes a church.

We agree, it is time to be done with a Christian culture that breeds narcissists for senior leaders and passive spectators for members.

These houses of peace are just the beginning. It seems that emotionally mature spiritual moms and dads are God's plan for building and nurturing this relational revolution.

But as we have trained, we have asked God, “What is the end result?”

The answer: Ecosystems of Grace—healthily bonded, intergenerational, uniquely designed groups of people who together embody the presence of God in the world around them.

6

Nurturing Ecosystems of Grace

Declaration 5

We are a group of uniquely gifted individuals who celebrate our differences. We learn from, and honor, every person we meet because we know they are also image-bearers of God. The more we are curious and pay attention to the hearts of others, the more God's image emerges. As we discover our unique design, we are able to connect more fully with others, appreciating all that they bring so that we can go further together. As we nurture life and co-create with each other, we get to see the multifaceted wisdom of God emerge in all of the Trinity's fullness.

As each gifted child of God matures in love and learns to bring their unique personality, design, and gifts to bear with their community for the needs of their world, a whole ecosystem of God's love forms. This becomes a compelling witness to the world that God is indeed here with us. Amazingly, this "manifold (multifaceted) wisdom of God" revealed through the church is even a witness to the rulers and authorities in the heavenly realms, which, according to Paul, was God's eternal purpose.[66]

An ecosystem in biology is an interdependent community of living organisms such as humans, animals, plants, and microbes that share resources in common. A healthy ecosystem involves high degrees of unique giftedness as well as a strong linking together of these highly differentiated organisms. Differentiation and linkage are necessary. Wholeness is uniqueness and togetherness, existing in an interdependent, joy-filled dance of giving and receiving that flows into regenerative life.

When emotionally mature human community is happening, these whole ecosystems of God's grace become demonstration plots of God's love and multifaceted wisdom. Uniquely designed individuals connect together to train in their skill and grow in their relational maturity. They share their hearts with each other, and they stream God's consistent presence so powerfully that people know there is something different about them.

Wholeness is uniqueness and togetherness, existing in an interdependent joy-filled dance of giving and receiving that flows into regenerative life.

---

[66] Eph. 3:10-11

In this type of community, God's presence (Father, Son and Spirit) emerges in all of its uniqueness and diversity. Such communities are undeniable evidence that God's life of love is not just wishful thinking. God does indeed dwell among us.

Here's how Jesus said it:

Love one another as I have loved you. In this, people will know you are my disciples—by the quality of your love for one another.[67]

This shared love, sourced in God's own life, is the good news with skin on, right here, right now. The essential marker of such communities of love is the belief in, and the free exercise of, every person's design and gifting, whether that person is a 6-year-old boy or a 92-year-old woman. This is what a vibrant family of Jesus looks like.

Such families have the lifestyle and commitment to nurture each person in the unique calling God gives them. So, what is this calling and how do we find it? Not surprisingly, it starts with God. God calls us together out of captivity and darkness to participate in God's own life. This is what the *ekklesia* is–literally, "the called-out community of God."

This calling comes to each of us in two forms:

- The call that all of God's people receive, that is, the grace-gifts we share in common

---

[67] John 13:34-35

- The particular callings that come to us as individuals and as communities that are specific to our situations.

The writer of Ephesians unpacks this distinction between universal and particular calling as he urges his readers to "therefore, live a life aligned with the calling to which you have been called."[68] As he continues, the author names first the universal gifts all God's people have received: "one Body, one Spirit, one hope, one Lord, one faith, one baptism, one God and Father of all."[69]

At this point, the focus shifts to the particular calling of each person. "But to each one of us a grace has been given as distributed by Christ."[70] Certain gifts of leadership and influence are given, but these are for the explicit purpose of calling forth, drawing out the gifting of each member of the body.[71]

As every member's gift is released, people become God's human gifts to the world and the eternal purposes of God in Christ are realized:

From Christ the whole body is joined and held together...by means of the distributed divine energy of

[68] Eph 4:1
[69] Eph 4:4-6
[70] Eph 4:7
[71] This whole constellation of thought concerning calling stands in contrast to the widely-held American notion that "you can be anything you want to be."

every single growing part of the body working to build up his body in love.[72]

How does such a community actually come together? It emerges when mature spiritual adults, led by Jesus, create the space for each person to discover and exercise their own design and gifts. The work of biological parents is to call forth the maturation and gifting of their own children. The work of spiritual parents is to call forth the maturation and gifting of the whole community.[73]

These human gifts, like all of God's gifts, are an invitation into God's joy: the delight of being glad to be together. Calling is an invitation to this God-joy, that brings joy not only to us but for the whole world. It is not only a grace-gift *by* which we are saved but also a grace-gift *for* which we are saved. As Frederick Buechner put it, "The place

---

The work of biological parents is to call forth the maturation and gifting of their own children. The work of spiritual parents is to call forth the maturation and gifting of the whole community.

---

[72] Eph 4:16

[73] The grace (*charis*) that each disciple receives, along with the corresponding equipment to fulfill that grace (*charismata*) is a repeated, commonly assumed theme elsewhere in the New Testament. See, for example, Rom 12:3–8 and 1 Pet 4:10, Eph 4:11-12.

God calls you to is the place where your deep gladness and the world's deep hunger meet."[74]

This gift of joy-infused individuals called out together by God in a particular place and time becomes God's custom-made demonstration plot–an ecosystem of grace. This is a playground for God's life on display, here and now.

When such communities are available to everyone, everywhere, God's plan to fill all the earth with God's own life will be complete. The Bride of Christ will be ready. Then, as Jesus said, the end of this age comes–an end that marks the beginning of a new age of deeper joy. As the prophet promised, "the Glory of the Lord will fill the earth as the waters cover the sea."[75]

The Cultural Shift

To see the multifaceted character of God emerge in the community requires that we see each other as God-carriers, people made in God's image. All people carry God's image, even those who do not believe in or know God. And those of us who receive Christ's love offering get to experience the living God dwelling inside of us in the form of the Holy Spirit. When we see each other through this lens, we are curious about each other; we draw out God's presence from each other; we learn from each other; we are humble with each other, and we celebrate differences.

---

[74] Frederick Buechner, *Wishful Thinking: A Seeker's ABC* (New York: Harper and Row, 1984), 119
[75] Habakkuk 2:14

The ways this multifaceted character of God played out in early Christian homes is clearly seen in 1 Corinthians 14:26. This verse describes what happened when Christians gathered. Notice particularly the word "everyone." Everyone contributed. Everyone had a voice. There were no mere spectators.

What shall we say, brothers? When you come together, everyone has a hymn, or a word of instruction, a revelation, a tongue or an interpretation. All of these must be done for the strengthening of the church (or called out ones).

Church in the first century was highly participatory. It was truly the priesthood of all believers at work![76]

In many people's experience with church, the only ones who have a voice are those who have the most knowledge of the scriptures. We have to let go of this value because God has deeply anointed some of the "least of these" with incredible insight and wisdom that comes from an interactive connection with God. Our children teach us just as much as our learned elders.

Church in the first century was highly participatory. It was truly the priesthood of all believers at work!

---

[76] 1 Peter 2:5-9

Unfortunately, many of us live in toxic shame that cripples us and keeps us from sensing God's presence inside us. We are taught that our hearts are wicked and sinful and that nothing good can dwell there.

Yet we are God-bearers. And as believers, God has given us a new heart; God's Spirit resides with us. We are loved, desired, valued, and delighted in. "While we were yet sinners, Christ died for us."[77]

And together, as our hearts, our design, and our gifts are drawn out, a fullness of God's presence emerges among us that is more complete. We see God when we see the reflection of God in the eyes of each other.[78]

Understanding that we see God in each other's eyes means that "church" cannot simply be a service where there are few leaders and many spectators. This cannot only be about intellectually believing the right things and trying hard to live them out. While there is value in good teaching and large group worship, this is not the full essence of the New Testament church.

Church, *ekklesia*, "the called-out community of God," for us has become emotionally healthy family relationships, educing the gifts, the God-design and the calling from each other.[79] We then link together, listening to Jesus for our next steps in seeking and saving all that was lost in ourselves, in each other, and in the world around us. This

---

[77] Romans 5:8

[78] For more on this see *Becoming a Face of Grace* by Ed Khouri.

[79] Educe means to draw out something hidden or latent.

can be in groups as small as two or three and can only grow at the speed of healthy attachment. Every heart has become paramount in this cultural shift, and every person is important.[80]

[80] Mt. 18:20

7

Creating New Culture

God is raising up a network of joy-fueled, Jesus-led communities of practice that are equipping spiritual parents to nurture ecosystems of grace. God is using these five values of this relational revolution to invite us into a new culture that is really as old as the first band of people Jesus called to "Follow me."

While for some of us, God's invitation seems like a "new way," in reality it is not new, only forgotten. Over the course of Christian history, God has steadily called for shifts or reforms in the religious culture of the day. Jesus walked this path himself, and his earliest followers challenged the religious norm for centuries.

As the Roman empire began to make the church a tool of the state in the early 300's, spiritual mothers and fathers gathered communities of practice in the desert. Farther north, Celtic Christian men and women formed vibrant communities that renewed the church and brought good news to a re-paganized Europe. Names we know: Francis and Clare, Hus, Wycliffe, Spener, Zinzendorf, Wesley.

We have seen God challenging a head-centered, love-starved Christian culture and inviting us to join him in rediscovering what it means to be his "called out community" marked by...love.

God only knows the many who have led the Relational Revolution that will never make the history books.

Such a time is once again upon us. Over the last twenty years, we have seen God challenging a head-centered, love-starved Christian culture and inviting us to join him in rediscovering what it means to be his "called out community" marked by a qualitatively different life of love.

We who are "done" with church as we have known it are reconsidering the whole of Christian culture, including what we have held dear in the past. It was our *stories*, *settings* and *systems* which led to the ineffective "pastor-led, program-centric, building-based culture of church that is so predominant in the US today."[81] And as our longing for more continues, we have sensed God inviting us to re-exam these elements of culture in which we have found ourselves. That is what we have attempted to do.

---

[81] *The State of the Church in America*

Now, we tie it all together.

Our Stories

The kind of culture change we're seeing starts with the stories we tell: *The* Story, *My* Story, *Our* Story and *This* Story.

The Story is the one that begins in joy and ends in deeper Joy. It is God's story, the alternative story. It is the whisper we all heard saying, "Come, share in our delight!"

The new culture gets personal as we embrace *My* Story, God's call on my own life through design and gifting, the realities of my personal experience and my own invitation to the new life of following Jesus.

But there's more. My gifts and calling truly begin to find their place as they are drawn forth, practiced and exercised in a vibrant family of Jesus: *Our* Story.

In this community of God's love, over time we become our truest selves and together are called by God into *This* Story–an ecosystem of God's living good news meeting the world's deep need, here and now.

As we have sought to create new practices that embody the values of this revolution, they have included regularly sharing these stories with each other, stories of appreciation and gratitude as we learn to listen to each other's hearts and God's heart for the world around us.

Our Setting

"Your Kingdom come…on earth as it is in heaven." That vision challenges us to pay attention to the *setting* of the new culture to which we are called. The first invitation of Jesus into this new lifestyle came in the villages of Galilee, along the dusty roads of Judea, right in the middle of the Roman occupation of the Jewish homeland.

We are not disembodied spirits or parasites on a planet, so God's call always comes in a physical context including natural surroundings as well as human-made dwellings. Our setting of time and place shapes our stories and therefore informs our practices.

One hundred and fifty years ago, people were generally well connected within family systems and regularly practiced relating. At the same time, they were largely isolated from the wider world. In that setting, gathering for a teaching/preaching time met needs at many levels.

Today, however, we can download excellent teaching from the best pastors all over the world and read the Bible every day, yet we are hard-pressed to find someone to look us in the eye and share their heart with us. People are typically disconnected and lonely and often suffer from any number of mental health issues. As we look at our current setting, we see that the practices we need are very different from those of 150 years ago.

Our Systems

While the culture humans shape together takes place through stories and occurs in particular settings, it is lived out in our *systems* of shared practice, sometimes called "liturgies". These systems are inherited and mostly unnoticed until they stop working well. Every family has systems or liturgies, as does every church body.

Simply put, these are the regular practices, habits, or rituals we use to affirm our values and frame the meaning of our lives. They are meant to help us connect to each other and to God…but over time, if not re-examined, they can actually prevent us from achieving that purpose.

The easiest parts of the system to recognize are usually the agreed-upon *rhythms* of our life together—when, where, and how we gather, play, pray, and work together. For a family, these include things like having meals together, praying before the meals, reading a bedtime story, what we do for holidays. For traditional church culture, it includes meeting times and even the order of service.

Most of the other aspects of our systems are harder to notice, but have shaped us in such profound ways that we must pay attention to their impact. *Covenants* and *communication* are two of these. *Covenants* are the agreements we have about who we are and why we are here together. *Communication* includes how we speak with each other, how we listen (or choose not to listen) not only to words, but also to the heart. Learning to communicate well helps us keep the relationships bigger than the conflicts.

Most importantly, we have to reimagine the vital question of how we make decisions together. How we *govern* ourselves as a family and/or a larger community has the power to fuel these five core values of the Kingdom of God or undermine them. In our time, our inherited systems of governance have brought division and power struggles to God's people. We must employ better ways to govern together.

People live unavoidably in a culture shaped by these dimensions of life: *Story*, *Setting* and *System.* While as children we may not be aware of our surroundings or the story we find ourselves in, as we mature and grow in relationship with our parents and the larger community, they hopefully guide us in understanding our family culture and larger community dimensions so we can eventually shape our own families, organizations, and communities.

How we govern ourselves as a family and/or a larger community has the power to fuel these five core values of the Kingdom of God or undermine them.

As Christians, we too are all born into a story, a setting, and a system that has been passed down to us. It is evident that God is inviting the elders of the Church today to pay radical attention to what he wants us to know about these dimensions of our culture. We do this not by trying to figure it all out with our own striving, but by listening to

Jesus together around new systems and practices that will actually empower us to follow God into the new "together life" that is the good news of God, here and now.

Don't you hear the whisper?

Don't you want to say *yes*?

8

The Invitation From Here...

Are you experiencing it?

The Life of God is coming. The Life of God is here.

Jesus taught us to pray, "Your Kingdom come, your will be done on earth as it is in heaven." That prayer has not gone, and will not go, unanswered.

Jesus himself initiated God's answer as he, and then his followers, formed the first vibrant families of Jesus. In the centuries that followed, as their opponents observed, they turned the ancient Roman world, "upside down."

And so, it has gone ever since. Wherever the seeds of God's love have found the soil of beloved community, a revolution of God's life has sprung up in that place.

Vibrant families of Jesus are forming all around us. These families are not only possible—they are necessary, in fact, they are inevitable.[82]

Are you sensing the call to "Come" and share in the delight of the original vibrant family, even as it means deconstructing much of the Christian culture you have known? Are you open to rediscovering the life of God that is here and is coming?

This new–old revolution is well underway. People around the world are being transformed by this ancient but always new culture inaugurated by Jesus. In this revolution, people are once again finding the invitation of Jesus to be such good news that they are ready to drop everything to get in on it.

God is using many organizations to awaken, inspire and equip those who are responding to the relational call. LK10 is one of them. Below we share a little more about who we are as well as what our unique contribution is to the revolution underway. The LK10 Community offers you camaraderie and equipping as you journey towards

---

God is using many organizations to awaken, inspire and equip those who are responding to the relational call. LK10 is one of them.

---

[82] Rev 7:9

nurturing communities that have at their core healthy attachment with God and each other. You can sign up to begin your training at LK10.com/next.

In the "Additional Resources" section, those we have learned from share more about who they are and how they uniquely participate to fuel the relational reorientation the church finds herself in today. Because of what these organizations offer, many leaders are now able to follow God into the cultural shifts necessary to see the church become the life and love of God once again.

Are you sensing the invitation to something more? Are you longing for God's presence to be manifest in you and those around you? Are you done with burnout, guilt and duty, functional Deism and spectator faith? Are you ready to join the relational revolution that is underway, taking "church" back into our relationships as families, friends, co-workers, neighbors?

If so, the next step is yours, "Come, share in our delight!"

The relational revolution is coming.

The relational revolution is here!

Books Are Okay...

But we believe this revolution is happening in communities of practice.

If you're interested in exploring LK10's training pathway further, visit LK10.com/next.

We've developed a training pathway that happens in safe, transformational groups, strengthening the spiritual and relational skills to lead yourself, your family, your community, your church or network.

If you are ready to move beyond this book's information, and into whole-life, whole-community transformation, get started with us today at LK10.com/next.

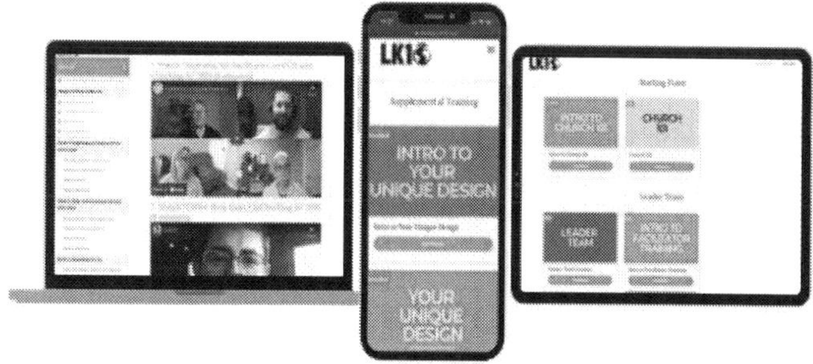

Resources and Unique Contributions

In addition to LK10, those whom we have learned from share more about who they are and how they uniquely participate to fuel the relational reorientation the church finds herself in today. We deeply appreciate these people and their contributions!

Vision is to see a vibrant family of Jesus in close reach of everyone on the planet. We see this as God's vision for the consummation of history: everything aligned under the lordship of Jesus.

Mission is to connect and equip maturing spiritual parents (leaders) who can nurture this revolution–this culture of God's arriving Kingdom.

LK10's unique contributions to this revolution:

Church of Two (CO2) or Church of Few: We train people to connect heart-to-heart with God and at least one other person in a simple, viral, participatory way that spontaneously builds the nineteen relational brain skills without people even knowing what a brain skill is![83]

As micro churches of two or three, we can practice loving God and each other every day![84] Our love-capacity grows exponentially because we practice daily. It is so simple that those as young as four years old can learn to be church together and yet so challenging that we can spend our whole lives deepening our practice.

---

[83] For a complete discussion on the nineteen relational brainskills, see *Transforming Fellowship: 19 Brain Skills that Build Joyful Community* by Chris Coursey

[84] Ecc. 4:9-12

Sometimes we call these tiny expressions of church "CO2s" for "churches of two." We are experiencing that when these CO2s are the first and most foundational expression of church, every other expression becomes more vibrant and mature. While forming and training churches of few is our niche, we do not stop with micro expressions. As God leads we gather in communities of practice, larger families, community groups and tribes.

Communities of Practice (Leader Teams): Designed for those wanting to continue their relational training, a Leader Team is a group of six to eight people meeting twice a month to mutually learn from and care for each other. We have found that lifelong Christian leaders who have healthy relational connections many times still lack the ability to create spaces where mutual discipleship can happen. They have never been trained to facilitate group learning in a way that allows Jesus to lead. In the past, many of us were trained in teaching groups or discipling individuals, but rarely taught to give and receive life with a band of skilled friends. In LK10's Leader Teams, we teach people how to disciple the group together as a whole. A well-discipled group is highly effective at discipling the individuals in the group, and the responsibility never falls solely on one person. We specialize in this type of training.

***Facilitator Training*:** For those who want to nurture groups of all sizes and serve as spiritual mothers and fathers, we provide apprentice-style facilitator training. This training equips people to facilitate every level of engagement in a way that is joy fueled, Jesus led, and draws out the multifaceted presence of God in the people gathered. We do this through hands on discovery learning and mentoring. Facilitators are observed and debriefed and are equipped to reproduce their skills in those around them.

In our Facilitator Training, we form facilitators who can effectively and consistently facilitate from a Joy-fueled, Jesus-led paradigm. Our LK10 facilitators feel resourced, equipped, and confident that they have what it takes, no matter what.

Find more information at LK10.com/next.

Life Model Works

Vision: Everyone who encounters the church is transformed into the image of Christ

Mission: To equip existing networks to create identity trans-formation into the likeness of Christ in church and culture

Unique Contribution: Life Model Works is committed to seeing individuals in a healthy relationship with God, self, and others. Our goal is to provide tools to the Christian community that not only restore our God-given identity, they make this restoration contagious. We've based these tools on the deepest understanding we can provide of God, creation and redemption.

Find more information at https://lifemodelworks.org/

THRIVEtoday/ Chris and Jen Coursey, thrivetoday.org

Vision: We want to see relationships thrive.

Mission: At THRIVEtoday we train individuals, families and communities in relational skills that can be used with God and each other.

Unique Contribution: THRIVEtoday is an application of the Life Model. We educate people to see the need for important, brain-based character skills. We equip people through stories of transformation and interactive exercises so people acquire new skills they've never had before and strengthen existing skills.

We do this with in-person trainings and resources such as books, videos, online groups and Habit Builder courses. These opportunities help people learn and spread relational skills into the fabric of their communities to reflect Christ relationally in the good and hard times of life.

Find more information at:
https://thrivetoday.org/freewebinars/

Immanuel Approach, for emotional healing and for life:

Vision: Every Christian (and eventually every person on the planet) experiences regular interactive connections with the tangible, living, loving, life-giving, friendship presence of God as a normal part of their everyday lives. And as they interact with God, and work with God to find and resolve hindrances between their hearts and Him, they increasingly grow secure attachment with the Lord.

Mission: To train as many people as possible to perceive God's living presence, to have regular, contingent, personal interactions with Him, and to find and resolve blockages that hinder an even better connection with God.

Unique Contribution: The Immanuel Approach focuses on a handful of principles and techniques, based on brain science and biblical truth, that help a recipient establish an interactive connection with the tangible, living, loving presence of God, and then help the person engage directly with the Lord regarding their questions, needs,, issues, problems, and trauma.

Find more information at

https://www.immanuelapproach.com/getting-started/

Eden Center for Regenerative Culture

Vision: A vibrant family of Jesus. A joyful, interdependent, intergenerational community of God's love and purpose, in close reach of everyone worldwide.

Mission: to be a vibrant family of Jesus ourselves and to equip others to cultivate these regenerative ecosystems of God's love in their own lives.

Unique Contribution: The Eden Center team is an incubator community that equips people to discover the unique calling of God on their own lives through deep attention to the Stories, Settings and Systems in which they live. Over time this empowers people to form a lifestyle of love in community across all the dimensions of their culture: economic, ecological and social. Love as a lifestyle is the goal—sharing together in the Life of God. Training is available to individuals, groups, churches and nonprofits through consultation and a variety of learning experiences.

Find more information at https://www.edencenter.org

Acknowledgements

John

I'm deeply grateful to my mother who celebrated her 100th birthday shortly before publishing this book. A church-goer her whole life, she has, in recent years, joined the ranks of the Dones. She's ready for a new church culture and is a big supporter of LK10. She is also my biggest cheerleader. It's been a delight to talk over this manuscript with her. Thanks, Mom!

Working on this book with Toni and Kent has been an amazing journey. Our personalities are very different which, at times, resulted in spirited disagreements about what to say and how to say it. Thankfully, we've learned to work through those disagreements by listening deeply to each other and to Jesus. I count each of them as a dear friend. I am so glad to be living out this relational revolution with them.

Toni

I want to thank our entire LK10 community, especially those who labored over this manuscript, submitting feedback and helping us better communicate who we are and what we are experiencing. Your feedback was essential Sarah Harrington, Travis Woronowicz, Steven Rice, Tom Gordon, Byron Parson, Neil Bradshaw, Leah and Ryan Nenaber, Carine Merhi, Wendy Cohen, Colleen Caskey, Lamar and Inell Claypool, Julie McKnight, Tom Prichard,

George Leonard, Paul Chierico, Susan Ramsey, Jen Hamilton, and Jim Mellon.

I also want to thank John and Kent for committing to live these values out in our relationship with each other. It has been a deep, transformative privilege that has rounded my edges while simultaneously empowering me to step into all the fullness of who I am meant to be. My family thanks you as well ;-)

Special thanks go to my husband, Matt, and my two youngest children (teens at the writing of this book) who are crazy enough to put heart-to-heart connection above all else. Life would be incredibly lonely without your love and daily support.

Kent

If it is true that we are formed most by those we love and who love us, then I am truly a blessed man. My father, Dale, and mother, Mary Jo–whom we lost as this book was coming together–have been my first and most enduring mentors in the life of love.

My bride, Karen, our five children and eleven grandchildren are my steady trainers in giving and receiving love. Our spiritual family in the Eden Community is a living demonstration to me that the life of love Jesus promised is no pipe dream, but a priceless and possible way of life.

And my amazing friends and collaborators in LK10: John, Toni and the whole team keep alive in me the hope that we can all participate–wherever we are found by God–in a Vibrant Family of Jesus.

To each of these, and most of all, to the God who is our very source of Love, I give my deep thanks.

From all of us: A special thank you to Zach LaValley and Hilary Kline for heading up the launch of this book using the courses from Selfpublishing.com.

Read More

We are in the process of writing books that expound on each of the five values of the Relational Revolution (Joy Fueled, Jesus Led, Communities of Practice, Spiritual Parents, Ecosystems of Grace). Joy Fueled is already available!

Our next book on being Jesus Led will be coming SOON!

Sign up at LK10.com/bookupdate

to get notified when it is released.

Author Bios

Video of authors introducing each other: https://www.youtube.com/watch?v=Yd2xNLaTONY

JOHN C WHITE is the host of the podcast, "Stories of the Revolution", a spiritual entrepreneur and Co-founder of LK10 with the vision of seeing "Vibrant families of Jesus in easy access of every person in every region and people group on earth."

John is a graduate of Washington and Lee University (BA in Sociology) and Fuller Seminary (MDiv). Following seminary, he served as an ordained Presbyterian pastor (EPC) in three churches over the course of 25 years in Denver, CO. In 1998, the Lord moved him out of the institutional church world and into the fledgling world of house churches. In that context, he served as a house church coach and as US Coordinator with DAWN Ministries for 6 years

As the LK10 Vision Champion, John was the original designer of both the Church 101 Course and Leader 101.

Since 2008, those Courses have been responsible for training more than 5000 people in 30 countries in the skills necessary for forming, nurturing, and reproducing vibrant families of Jesus. John can currently be found training, coaching, and facilitating live video calls and connecting with leaders around the world on the latest messaging apps.

John and his wife, Tamela, enjoy their three grandkids, playing tennis, and eating the delicious Albanian food Tamela cooks. While they have lived in Denver, CO for most of their married lives, they recently moved to Naples, FL for the warm weather and to be closer to family. They will however, still be rooting for the Denver Broncos! John can be reached at John.LK10@gmail.com and through his Podcast "Stories of the Revolution".

TONI M DANIELS lives to see relational restoration in every level of society by awakening, inspiring, and training emotional, spiritual ninja warriors who follow Jesus into his revolution of joy. To that end, she has authored several books and is the host of the podcast "Joy Fueled and Jesus Led."

Before settling stateside, Toni founded Godly Play Uruguay and worked alongside her husband, Matt, as a social entrepreneur, church planter, and relational coach, starting churches and founding a leadership training center.

In her role as LK10's Operations and Training Champion, Toni has created training pathways for hundreds of global leaders to form healthy attachments by nurturing vibrant families of Jesus.

Toni earned a BA in Spanish and Sociology. She has an MA in Leadership Development and Church Planting, a diploma in Spiritual Direction, and five years of relational skills-based training from the International Trainer's Association, PREP, Inc., and THRIVEToday.

Toni loves building joy with family and friends. Her hobbies include karaoke, quilting, and kayaking. Toni currently resides in Nashville, TN.

DR. P. KENT SMITH is a visionary community developer who co-founded both LK10 and the Eden Community, where he has found companionship in his quest to rediscover God's call to a life of love in our disconnected times.

In his early years, Kent began asking, "How can people in our time actually experience the lifestyle of love in community promised by Jesus?" His search for answers led him from undergraduate studies in Biology to a master's degree in New Testament, and finally to a doctorate on Spiritual Nurture Systems. Along the way, he led several new and established churches.

In 1991 Kent joined the faculty of Abilene Christian University and began training domestic and overseas mission teams. After a year in Oxford, England in 2002, he became the founding director of ACU's graduate internship in missional leadership, the Missionary Residency for North America (MRNA). In 2008, Kent co-founded LK10 where he serves as overseer and Ecosystem Champion.

Kent and his wife Karen have five children and eleven grandchildren. They enjoy gardening, writing, research, travel and their shared work with the Eden Community of coaching students and consulting with new kingdom community initiatives across North America. Kent can be reached at kent.smith@acu.edu

Would You Review?

Help Get the Word Out!

Thank you for reading
***Relational Revolution*!**

We really appreciate all of your feedback and love hearing what you have to say.

Your review can help this book get into the hands of others who are searching for words to describe the longings of their hearts.

Also, all proceeds go to LK10.com, so your review is an incredible way to contribute to the Relational Revolution!

Please take two minutes now to leave a helpful review on Amazon letting us know what you thought of the book:

LK10.com/review

Thanks so much!

LK10

Made in the USA
Middletown, DE
03 April 2024

52529535R00073